STAN
MUSIAL

Library of Congress Control Number: 2015957548

ISBN: 9781681060361

Design by Jill Halpin

Printed in the United States of America
16 17 18 19 20   5 4 3 2 1

STAN
MUSIAL

CONTENTS

★ CHAPTER ★
ONE

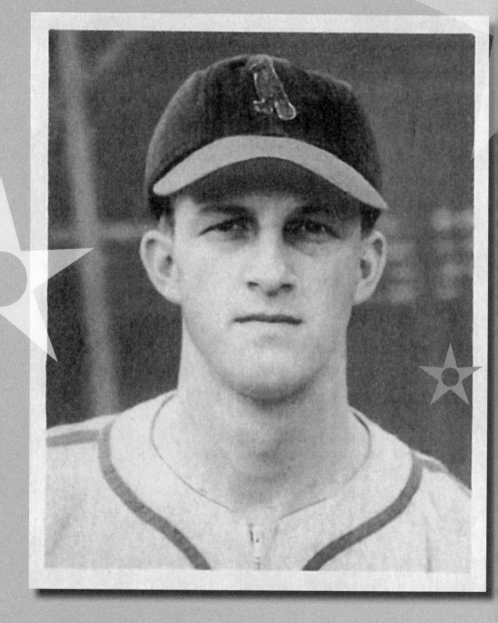

The little boy tossed a ragged black ball into the air. Up it sailed and down it fell, back in the boy's hands. Up and down the ball flew as the boy walked. Neighbors smiled and waved. Some shouted, "Hey Stashu!" Everybody in Donora, Pennsylvania, knew the boy with the ball. He was Stanislaw Musial and he was baseball crazy.

Stan was born November 21, 1920, and grew up during the Great Depression. Jobs were hard to find and money was scarce. People who lived in Donora were grateful for jobs in the dirty black coal mines and grimy factories. At least they could buy food for their family.

Stan's dad worked long hours at the wire mill, but it didn't pay very much. Stan's mom and his four sisters had to get jobs doing cooking and laundry to earn extra money. Stan and his brother dug coal from a pit near their home, and used the coal to heat their house. There was barely enough money for food at the Musial house. A store-bought baseball was a luxury Stan couldn't imagine.

But Stan's mother understood how much he loved baseball so she made him balls out of rocks, rags, and tape. A small pebble was at the center of the ball with strips of cloth wound round and round until it was the size of a baseball. Then Stan's mom stitched the ball together. If she could afford to, she covered it in black electrical tape. That made the ball last longer. They were heavier than a store-bought ball, but Stan didn't care. He had a baseball. He could play.

Whenever Stan had free time, he roamed the hilly streets of Donora looking for anyone willing to start up a baseball game. The kids played in empty lots and in the city park. Mining had stripped the hills of trees and a cloud of coal soot hung in the sky even on sunny days. That didn't matter to Stan. All he cared about was throwing, hitting, and catching the baseball.

At first the older boys refused to let Stan play with them. They didn't want a skinny little kid messing up their game. But Stan was persistent. He hung around until someone hit a foul ball, then he would chase it down and throw it back. The older boys were amazed that a little kid could throw so well. They decided to give him a chance. Soon Stan was chasing down balls in the outfield, and learning how to hit a curve ball.

Stan's dad had grown up in Poland and didn't know how to play baseball, but his neighbor was Joe Barbo. Joe was an accomplished ballplayer and manager of a semi-

DONORA,
WASHINGTON COUNTY, PENNSYLVANIA.
1901.

4

pro team called the Donora Zink Works. He took a liking to young Stan and invited him over to play catch and listen to the Pittsburgh Pirates games on the radio. Stan soaked up every bit of advice Joe had to give, and asked Joe to teach him how to pitch.

On warm summer evenings the sound of the radio announcer echoed in the yard as Stan threw until his left arm ached. Joe shouted instructions and cheered as Stan improved. Sometimes they took a break to drink iced tea and talk about their favorite players.

Lefty Grove was Stan's idol. He played for the Philadelphia Athletics, and was one of the best left-handed pitchers in history. Stan dreamed of being a famous left-handed pitcher like Lefty Grove. He spent hours practicing his pitching, imagining that he was on the mound facing big league hitters just like Lefty. The more Stan practiced, the better he got.

Baseball wasn't the only sport Stan played. When his father was a child in Poland all the boys learned gymnastics, and he enrolled Stan and his younger brother in the Polish Falcons Gymnastics Club. The boys spent winter afternoons learning to somersault, flip, and tumble. Stan thought it was fun to fly through the air, and his muscles grew strong from working on the rings and bars. But the best thing he learned was how to fall without getting hurt. Stan knew to let his body stay loose and roll with the fall. All through grade school and high school Stan managed to avoid injuries because he knew how to fall.

By the time Stan got to high school, all of Donora knew his name. They cheered for him when he was play-

HIGH SCHOOL, DONORA, PA.

Donora High School where Stan attended Jr. High

ROBERT (LEFTY) GROVE

ing basketball, and they yelled for him when he was pitching for the Donora Zinc Works baseball team.

Stan's high school basketball team was so good that in 1938 they won their league tournament. With Stan dribbling down the court, Grant Gray on defense, and Florentino Garcia as a guard, they were a powerhouse team. They were excited to get to play in the state tournament at the University of Pittsburgh. Hundreds of people from Donora traveled to Pittsburgh to watch the team play. The boys were excited too. They got to eat out at a fancy restaurant and stay in a hotel, but they got a rude surprise at the Schenley Hotel.

The hotel manager refused to serve Grant Gray because he was African American. Stan and his teammates were angry. The boys on the team were from many different backgrounds: Spanish, Polish, Slova-kian, and African American. They felt it was wrong to discriminate against their friend because of his skin color. The team met with their coach and they all agreed that if Grant was not permitted to stay with them, they would leave and not play in the tournament.

After some meetings with the university officials and the coaches, the hotel agreed to change its policy and let Grant stay in the hotel. It was a victory Stan would remember for the rest of his life.

The summer of Stan's sophomore year, scouts from major league baseball began attending games in Donora

Donora High School basketball team (Stan, second from left)

to watch Stan play. The scouts described him as a tall, skinny kid with a strong arm and solid batting. They decided to keep an eye on Stan and see how he improved.

Lillian Labash was also in the stands cheering and keeping her eye on Stan. Lil was a tiny, bubbly girl with blonde hair and a big crush on the baseball and basketball star. Stan thought Lil was pretty cute and the two started going to school dances together. After ball practice, Stan would walk a mile into town to visit Lil. Lil thought Stan was more interested in the sandwiches and milk her mother served than in her. Lil's father owned a grocery store and Stan did enjoy a good slab of free lunch meat, but he also fell in love with the lovely Lillian Labash.

Besides being devoted to baseball and Lil, Stan was also devoted to his church. His family went to mass every Sunday and it was a practice he kept all his life, whether he was on the road or at home.

And going on the road started early for Stan. When he turned 16, the baseball scouts from the St. Louis Cardinals decided Stan was good enough to play for their

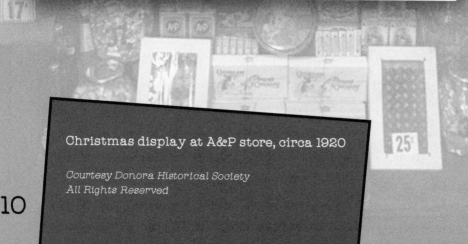

Christmas display at A&P store, circa 1920

Class D farm team. Stan couldn't believe his luck. He hadn't even graduated from high school and he had a chance to play professional baseball.

Stan's dad was not happy. He didn't think baseball could really be a career for Stan. He wanted him to go to college or learn how to work at the factory so he could earn money and support a family. Since Stan was under age, he had to have permission from his parents to sign the baseball contract. He was desperate. Baseball was his dream. He pleaded with his father to let him

Donora Zinc Works baseball team

this picture we present the members of -nora Zinc Works baseball team which is great "guns" this year in the Mononga- ley League, composed of ten clubs, large- uited from industries in that region. The s supported by the Donora Zinc Works Employe's Athletic Association. From left right, back row:- Koval. Hutchinson, Dekarski Captain Sala, Benyo, Trybuski, Durka, Musia Koskoski, Manager. Front row—left to right Donley, Relosky, Anders, Hostenski, Neidermeye Rodriguez, Mackiewicz, Kavalec.

try. He promised that he would finish high school. It was Stan's mother who finally talked his dad into signing the contract. She reminded Stan's father that he had come to America because he could do anything he wanted in America. Become anything. Didn't his son deserve the same opportunity?

Stan Musial was ready to live out his dream. At the end of his junior year of high school, he hopped on a bus full of strangers and rode 240 miles to Williamson, West Virginia. It was a long, hot ride and when he stepped off the bus, Stan realized it was the farthest he had ever been from home.

Stan's mom, Mary Lancos Musial
(middle back), circa 1915

THE 1920s

Imagine a world with no television, no computers, and no cell phones. Sounds kind of boring, right? But wait. It gets worse. There are no video games, many people still use outhouses, and they have to buy blocks of ice just to keep their food cold. This was what the world was like when Stan Musial was born in 1920.

Stan was born just two years after the end of the Great War (World War I). It was a time of great change. American men were returning from fighting in Europe and they had seen modern inventions in the cities of Paris and London. They liked having toilets in the house and driving motor cars. They were excited to try new inventions that could make their lives easier. And there were plenty of new inventions!

The electric refrigerator, washing machine, and vacuum were brand new in the 1920s, but they were so expensive that Stan's family could not afford such luxuries. Inventors also introduced electric irons, sunglasses, and the first traffic lights.

Thanks to Henry Ford and his assembly line, cars were starting to outnumber horses and traffic control was necessary.

There were also new inventions in health care. Band-Aids were introduced in the 1920s. Before that, scraped knees were wrapped in rags or covered with gauze and tape. And more important was the development of lifesaving medicines like penicillin and insulin.

But the one invention that probably mattered most to Stan and his friends was the invention of the radio. On November 2, 1920, just eighteen days after Stan was born, the first American commercial radio station started broadcasting. Located in Pittsburgh, Pennsylvania, just miles from Stan Musial's home, KDKA announced the winner of the presidential election. Warren Harding had beaten James Cox in the race for the White House.

Radio quickly became the center of entertainment for many families. Radio stations announced the successful flight of Charles Lindbergh over the Atlantic Ocean. They played music and eventually broadcast sports

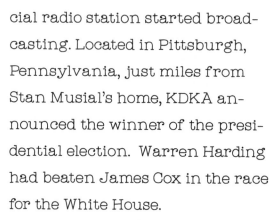

games, plays, and comedy shows. Families would gather around the radio to listen to the adventures of Amos and Andy, the music of the Grand Ole Opry, or the stories of the Mystery House.

By the time Stan was 12 years old, he could listen to regular broadcasts of the Pittsburgh Pirates ball games and hear the World Series on the radio. He could cheer the adventures of Tarzan and shiver at the mysteries of Charlie Chan. As he grew older, Stan would listen to President Franklin Roosevelt's fireside chats and learn how America would cope with the Great Depression and World War II. The radio brought Americans together and helped Stan and his friends appreciate the wonders of the United States and the world.

You can listen to the same programs that Stan and his friends enjoyed when you visit these websites: http://www.radio-lovers.com/pages/allshows.html http://www.oldradioworld.com.

16

★ CHAPTER ★
TWO

Stan was homesick. He missed the familiar craggy hills of Donora and walking to his friends' homes. He missed Lil and his family. He missed his mother's cooking. But he loved playing baseball. It was the best summer of his life.

Stan had so much to learn about being a professional player. He had a good fastball, but he was wild. The coaches worked with him to be more consistent and improve his control. He also had to learn about all the signs used by catchers in the major leagues and how to back up the bases. He learned about relay throws and cutoffs. He also learned how to live on his own.

His salary was $65 a month, and his boarding house cost $5 a week. Stan lived on a steady diet of hamburgers and hot dogs and managed to save some of his earnings to help out back home. At the end of the season he had a 6-6 win-loss record. Wid Matthews wrote up a scouting report on Stan for the Cardinals, and it said, "Arm good. Good fastball, good curve. Poise. Good hitter. A real prospect."

In the fall Stan did exactly what he promised his dad he would do. He packed up his ball and glove and returned to Donora to finish his senior year of high school. School was not Stan's favorite activity. He was a decent student but he would rather have been playing ball. He studied enough to make sure he would pass all of his classes, but his spare time was spent playing ball.

Since he had played professional sports, he was ineligible to play on any of the high school teams. Instead, he played basketball for a neighboring town's semipro team. His pay was mainly in the form of Italian food. Of course the way Stan could eat, it was probably a pretty good salary.

In the spring, he helped coach his high school baseball team and played for Joe Barbo's Zinc Works team. He studied just enough to make sure he would pass all of his classes and get his high school diploma. But when the Cardinals called him back to Williamson, he left before graduation day. Lil had to stand in for him at graduation and pick up his diploma.

When Stan arrived in Williamson in the summer of 1939, he received a raise to $75 per month. He was still pitching but had some trouble with soreness in his arm and wildness in his pitches. But his batting was impressive.

Stan's batting stance was distinctive. Some people might even say strange. He crouched low with his knees knocked together. One coach said he looked like a little kid peeking around a corner. But the stance worked for Stan. During the 1939 season he had a 9-2 pitching record and a .352 batting average. It was enough to earn Stan a raise to $100 a month for the 1940 season.

By the spring of 1940, war was raging in Europe. Germany had invaded Czechoslovakia and Poland. Britain, France, Australia, and New Zealand had all declared war on Germany. The newspapers were full of the stories of bombings and blitzes, and people in the United States wondered if their country would be able to avoid the conflict. Baseball was a wonderful distraction.

Now married, Stan and Lil spent the summer of 1940 in Daytona Beach. There Stan made a lifelong friend in manager Dickie Kerr. Kerr had played major league ball for the White Sox and like Stan he was a lefty. Kerr had won the respect of America in 1919 during the White Sox betting scandal. Eight of the White Sox players had agreed to try to intentionally lose the games. They were paid a large amount of money by professional gamblers who planned to make a profit because they "knew" which team would win the series.

But Dickie Kerr was not involved in the betting scandal. He worked hard to win the series despite the best players working against him. Kerr won both games he started, and threw one shutout. When news of the scandal broke, Kerr was remembered as being one of the good guys.

Dick Kerr
PITCHER, CHICAGO, AM.L.

Kerr and his wife, Corrine, offered to let the Musials live with them to help save on expenses. Lil was expecting their first baby in August and the young Musials were grateful for the help. Stan deeply respected Dickie Kerr and listened to his advice on baseball and life.

Under Kerr's guidance Stan was able to improve his pitching so that he pitched 18 winning games. His win-loss record for the season was 18-5, but he was still inconsistent and walked nearly as many players as he struck out.

When Stan wasn't pitching, Kerr experimented with having Stan play in the outfield. This kept him in the batting rotation and Stan's batting average that summer was an impressive .311. The Cardinal scouts were sending reports to the main office praising Stan's batting more than his pitching.

A graphic run by a newspaper in 1920 after the breaking of the Black Sox scandal.

Then two events changed his life forever. The first was the birth of his son Richard, named after Dickie Kerr. Stan and Lil were thrilled with their adorable new son. But in the same month his son was born, Stan fell and sustained a serious injury.

He was playing center field when a low line drive was hit his way. As he had done hundreds of times in the past, he charged and dived for the ball. He was used to somersaulting on the field; he had been trained by the Polish Falcons how to tumble and fall. But this time his spikes caught in the turf and he landed heavily on the point of his left shoulder—his pitching arm.

Pain rushed through Stan's arm and a knot rose on his shoulder. The next morning he had a series of X-rays. Stan

Stan with his mother, Mary, and wife, Lil, attending a dinner in his honor in 1957.

Stan and Lil in the kitchen,
Donora, Pennsylvania
(October 1943)

and Kerr were both relieved to see there were no broken bones. The doctors advised rest and Stan reluctantly agreed. But when Stan returned to the mound in September for the playoffs, his arm was weak. He couldn't throw as hard as before. Kerr put Stan in the outfield for the last game of the season. Stan was worried. This could mean the end of his baseball dreams.

That winter Stan and Lil decided to stay in Florida. The warm winter weather would allow Stan to practice outside and it might help his arm feel better. He got a job in the Sports Department at Montgomery Ward. He sold

23

24

golf clubs, baseball bats, and gloves. To save money, the Musials stayed with the Kerrs.

Stan spent many hours talking with Dickie about his future. What would he do if he couldn't pitch? Would the Cardinals let him go? Dickie told Stan to think about playing outfield and concentrating on his batting skills. Stan was open to the idea, but said he would let the Cardinals' managers decide where to put him.

In the spring of 1941 Hitler and his soldiers were marching across Europe destroying towns and villages, and filling concentration camps with dissenters, rebels, and Jews. The US Congress allowed America to sell war goods to Allied countries and ended their stance of neutrality. The United States had not officially joined in the war against Germany, but people worried that it was only a matter of time before young men like Stan would be sent to fight.

Stan was more worried about his baseball career. When he reported to spring training for the Columbus (Georgia) Redbirds, he quickly learned his pitching arm was dead. It didn't hurt, but he had no power. His days of throwing hard seemed to be over.

Luckily, Stan's manager, Burt Shotton, believed that even if Stan couldn't pitch, he could still be a ballplayer. Like Dickie Kerr, he thought Stan could be a good outfielder and an excellent hitter. Stan was willing to play any spot as long as he could be a professional ballplayer. He packed his bags and reported to Springfield,

Missouri, as the Springfield Cardinals newest outfielder. It was the best move Stan could have made.

He had a great season. The warm Missouri summer seemed to agree with him, and after a few weeks Stan was comfortable playing outfield. He dove for balls and zipped them back to the infield. As he became more confident in his new position, he began hitting. Not just singles—but doubles, triples, and home runs!

Springfield fans began crowding into the bleachers to watch Stan smash balls out of the park. One night he hit three home runs against the Topeka Owls. His batting average soared above .300. During 87 games in Springfield he hit 26 homers, 94 runs batted in (RBIs), and had a

Stan checks waybills at his off-season job in October 1943.

batting average of .397. Stan's manager was thrilled. He told Stan that with a couple more years of work, he'd be in the big leagues. Stan was grinning from ear to ear. If he just kept working hard, his dream might actually come true. He'd be a ballplayer in the major leagues.

One day late in July, Stan and some of his buddies were enjoying a day off by fishing in the White River. Between baiting their hooks and casting their lines, they talked about baseball. It was a quiet summer afternoon and the guys were enjoying the solitude, until a reporter from the local paper showed up. What in the world was he doing invading their fishing trip?

He wanted to get comments from Stan on how he felt about being called up to the Rochester Red Wings. Was he excited to be going to the International League, only one step below the majors? Stan rushed home where he found the message waiting for him. It was true. He was to report immediately to Rochester, New York.

Stan wowed the Rochester crowd by getting four hits in his very first game. He had two singles, a double, and a homer. The fans loved him. Stan stayed with the Rochester Red Wings all the way through their playoffs. He kept hitting like his bat was on fire, but it wasn't enough to help the Red Wings win. They lost in five games. Stan packed his bags and headed back to Lil and baby Dickie in Donora. It had been a great season.

On Sunday the Musials attended church with their family. Stan was exhausted from all the travel and ball games. He stretched out on the couch for a Sunday afternoon nap. It seemed like he had only been asleep for a few seconds when Lil shook him awake. What could possibly be that important?

Lil waved a piece of paper in Stan's face. It was a wire from the Cardinals. They wanted him to report to St. Louis. They needed his help in the fight for the National League championship. Stan had made it to the big leagues. The baseball-crazy kid's dream had come true!

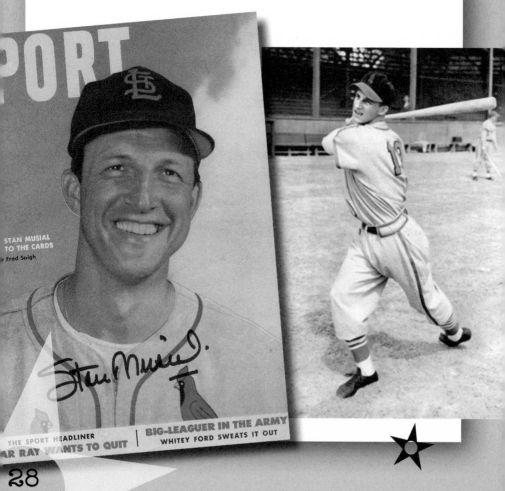

PORT

STAN MUSIAL
TO THE CARDS
y Fred Saigh

THE SPORT HEADLINER | BIG-LEAGUER IN THE ARMY
AR RAY WANTS TO QUIT | WHITEY FORD SWEATS IT OUT

DON'T QUIT YOUR DAY JOB

Salaries for professional athletes have increased a lot since Stan Musial was at bat. The Cardinals made newspaper headlines in 1958 when they offered Stan a record-breaking $100,000 one-year contract. He was the first player to receive a six-figure salary. It seemed like a fortune.

But compared to the salaries that today's top players make, Stan and his teammates were earning peanuts.

Taking inflation into account, Stan's six-figure salary would be worth over $800,000 in today's money. Still sounds like a lot of cash. But in 2015 the average major league player earned over $4 million dollars!

Top players earn five times that amount. Clayton Kershaw, a left-handed pitcher for the Los Angeles Dodgers, earned an annual salary of over $30 million in 2015. Justin Verlander earned over $25 million pitching for the Detroit Tigers, and Zack Greinke was paid over $24 million by the Dodgers. With salaries like that, major league players can spend the off-season exercising and staying in shape. It wasn't like that for Stan Musial.

Before the advent of television and advertising revenue, baseball players had to find ways to earn money in the off-season to keep their families fed and clothed. Some like Stan had ordinary jobs working in factories or clerking in stores. Yogi Berra and Whitey Ford both sold men's clothing in department stores. Ty Cobb was a farmer in Georgia, and Willie Mays sold cars in San Francisco. But some ballplayers had more unusual off-season careers.

When catcher Roy Campanella was playing for the Brooklyn Dodgers minor league team, he earned an unusual bonus. Baby chickens. A local farmer promised 100 baby chicks for every home

run. Roy hit 14 homers that season and earned himself 1,400 chickens. He didn't let a good bird go to waste and with the help of his father started a chicken farm that kept him busy in the off-season. Even when he made the big leagues, he continued to earn money from his chicks.

Pitcher Jim Turner helped the Yankees win the World Series in both 1940 and 1943, but when he wasn't on the mound he milked cows and then delivered the milk. Detroit Tigers third baseman Richie Hebner worked at his father's graveyard in the off-season digging graves. And when Ray Scarborough wasn't pitching for the Washington Senators, he was busy selling pickles.

Like Stan Musial, the players didn't complain about working during the off-season. They were just excited to have the chance to play professional baseball. They were all baseball crazy.

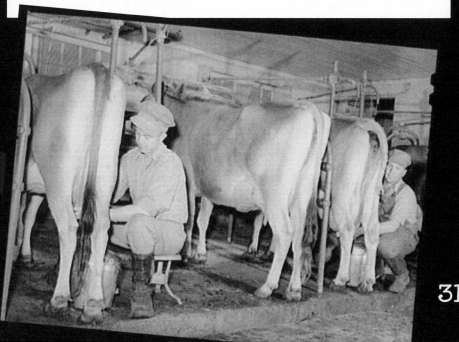

★ CHAPTER ★
THREE

September 17, 1941, was the day Stan Musial found his home. That morning he walked into Sportsman's Park in St. Louis for the very first time and fell in love with the St. Louis Cardinals. It was a match made in baseball heaven and one that would last a lifetime.

The Cardinals brought up three men from their farm teams to help them in the pennant race. With Stan that morning were Erv Dusak and George Kurowski. They were told to report to the equipment room for uniforms. The equipment manager rummaged through the spare uniforms trying to find something to fit the new recruits. He looked Stan up and down like a tailor sizing him up for a suit. Then he grabbed a uniform and tossed it to Stan.

Stan slipped on the uniform. It wasn't a perfect fit but it would work. On the back was the number that would be assigned to Stan Musial, the new Cardinal. It was number six. In over twenty years with the club, Stan never changed his number.

That afternoon, the Cardinals were scheduled to play a doubleheader against the Boston Braves. The manager started Stan in the second game. His first time up to bat Stan faced pitcher Jim Tobin. Tobin wound up and threw a knuckleball at the newbie. Stan had never faced a wobbly knuckleball and didn't know how to hit it. When his bat connected, he popped the ball up for an easy out. Stan felt like kicking himself. This wasn't the way he

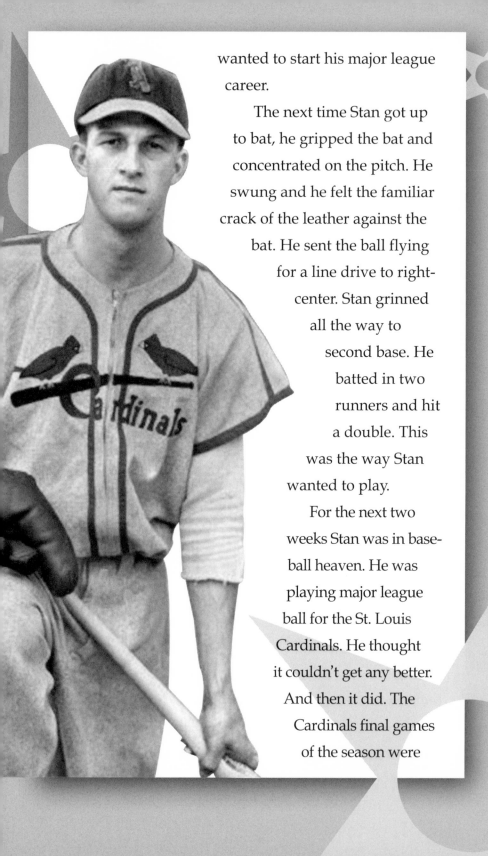

wanted to start his major league career.

The next time Stan got up to bat, he gripped the bat and concentrated on the pitch. He swung and he felt the familiar crack of the leather against the bat. He sent the ball flying for a line drive to right-center. Stan grinned all the way to second base. He batted in two runners and hit a double. This was the way Stan wanted to play.

For the next two weeks Stan was in base-ball heaven. He was playing major league ball for the St. Louis Cardinals. He thought it couldn't get any better. And then it did. The Cardinals final games of the season were at Forbes Field in Pittsburgh, just twenty-eight miles from Stan's hometown of Donora. Stan's family and friends were thrilled to be able to watch their home-town boy play in the major leagues. He managed to hit his first major league home run in front of his hometown supporters. Screaming and hollering, the fans showed their pride. The whole town of Donora celebrated with Stan. They gave the school-children the day off school, and declared it Stan Musial Day.

Stan was embarrassed by the hoopla, but grate-ful that so many people cared about him. He knew how much it meant for the kids to see that somebody from their small town could achieve their dreams. And one more of Stan's childhood dreams came true when he received a telegram from General Mills awarding him a case of Wheaties cereal.

It was an advertising gimmick used by General Mills to get attention for their cereal. Like most kids of the 1930s Stan had listened to the radio announc-ers say, "And for that home run a case of Wheaties will be shipped to . . ." This time, the Wheaties were headed for Stan.

The Cardinals gave it a good run, and won 97 games that season. But they were edged out of the pennant by the Brooklyn Dodgers, who won 100 games. Cardinal fans were disappointed, but Stan

was still riding high with a new contract in his pocket for the 1942 season.

On December 7, 1941, the whole world changed. The Japanese attacked Pearl Harbor and killed 2,403 Americans. They damaged all eight of the US Navy battleships and sank four of them. A stunned nation listened on the radio as President Roosevelt asked Congress to declare war on Japan. On December 11 Hitler declared war on the United States.

Young men across America volunteered for military duty. They wanted to serve and protect their country. Baseball players were no different. Many of the players were called into service by the mandatory draft that applied to all men ages 21 to 36.

Stan was exempt from the draft during the first few years of the war because he was the father of a young child and was supporting his parents with his income. Like everyone else, Stan wanted to do what he could to help. He knew that if the war lasted very long he would be called to fight. In the meantime, he used some of his savings to purchase war bonds to help finance the new ships and equipment the military needed.

The war caused many people to question whether or not there should even be a baseball season in 1942. During the First World War professional baseball games had been canceled, but President Roosevelt believed that baseball was good for the American spirit. It gave people something positive to talk about, and was a diversion from the grimness of war. He asked the team owners to go ahead with the season and said, "I honestly feel that it would be best for

the country to keep baseball going." Roosevelt also asked the managers to schedule more night games so that citizens who worked during the day could relax at a ball game.

That spring Stan reported for his first full season as a member of the St. Louis Cardinals. Because spring training was held in Florida, it was nicknamed the Grapefruit League for the fruit grown in the state. Stan was anxious to do well during training but his bat was cold. He had a few hits, but nothing to match the batting he had done the year before. Worried that he might have lost his touch, Stan felt like he was the "lemon of the Grapefruit League."

He told Lil to stay in Donora with her parents. He was nervous. What if he bombed? He didn't want to waste money paying for Lil to come and watch him fail. He had to improve.

Stan kept practicing long after other players had left the field. He took pitch after pitch, trying to get his batting rhythm going. He worked to swing the bat to meet the ball. Wood against leather. Muscle against bat. After a

USS *Shaw* exploding on December 7, 1941.

while his batting was smooth and strong. He felt like he had his swing back. And boy did he!

Once Stan got into the regular season, there was no stopping him. By the time the season ended, Stan had a .315 batting average, and he was batting cleanup for the Cardinals. He had 87 runs of his own, and 72 RBIs. Most exciting of all, Stan helped the Cardinals fight their way past the Brooklyn Dodgers to win the National League pennant. In his first full big league season, Stan was playing in the World Series.

The Cardinals were up against the New York Yankees. The "Bronx Bombers" had just won their thirteenth pennant and were the defending World Series champions. They had won five world championships in the last six years. The Yankees came to the series ready to send the Cardinals flying back to their nest in St. Louis.

The Cardinals were a young team. All of their players except one had been brought up through the Cardinals farm system. But the young Cardinals won an astonishing 106 games and they were excited to show the world they could beat the Yankee powerhouse.

Stan and his teammates were nervous. The first game was on their home turf at Sportsman's Park. The stands were packed with fans yelling and shouting. But the Cardinals didn't give them anything to cheer about. They went hitless for the first seven innings. The powerful Yanks had four runs to the Cardinals big fat zero.

Then it got worse. The Yankees scored three more runs. It was 7-0 in the ninth inning and the Yankees were feeling pretty good. Those young guys from the Midwest didn't have a chance against a baseball machine like the Yankees.

It was the bottom of the ninth, and the Yankees were already celebrating. Stan was up to bat. He wanted a hit in the worst way. The ball came toward him and Stan swung. His bat connected. The ball popped up and was immediately caught. Stan had fouled out. But Stan and the Redbirds weren't ready to give up.

Catcher Walker Cooper was next up to bat. He slugged a single. There was one man on base. First baseman Johnny Hopp flied out. There were two outs and one man on base. The Yankees only needed one more out to shut out the Cardinals. But amazingly, the Cardinals rallied and got five more hits. They drove in four runs. The game went from 7-0 to 7-4.

The bases were loaded and it was Stan's turn at bat. If he could hit a home run the Cardinals could actually win the game. The Yankees weren't celebrating anymore. Stan swung and his bat connected, but the ball grounded to first base and he was out. Stan was disappointed. He wanted to help win the game, and instead he had made the last out.

But back in the dugout, he found the Cardinals were excited. They may have lost the first game, but they had

44

showed the Yankees that they were a real threat. They were ready for the next game in the series. They knew they could beat the Yankees.

The next afternoon the Cardinals were playing in front of a packed stadium in St. Louis. Stan got his first hit in a World Series, and drove in the first run. Their fans cheered the team on to a 4-3 victory.

The next three games the Cardinals had to play in front of the Yankee fans in Yankee Stadium. It didn't bother the Cardinals. They beat the Yanks 2-0, 9-6, and 4-2. Stan and his teammates whooped and hollered. They pounded each other on the back and didn't stop shouting for an hour or more. They had won the Cardinals first World Series trophy since 1926.

Stan couldn't believe his luck. In his rookie season he had just played on a World Series–winning team. And he had been able to have his parents in the stands watching him. His father finally agreed that this baseball job might work out okay.

46

DECEMBER 7
1941

When Japan bombed Pearl Harbor on December 7, 1941, the world changed for Stan Musial and all of America. President Franklin Roosevelt announced on the radio that America was entering the war and would be fighting with the Allies against Germany, Austria, and Japan.

Stan was 21 years old and was required by law to register for service in the military. All men between the ages of 21 and 45 were required to register with the US government and when their name was picked they had to report for military duty. Every man had to have a physical examination

BUY WAR BONDS

to prove they were healthy enough to train and fight. The majority of men easily passed the physical, but some were exempted because of heart conditions, breathing problems, or other illnesses. Most men were eager to serve their country and fight to protect the United States. Those who refused to report to the military and ran away were considered draft dodgers. If they were caught, they were sent to jail. During World War II, ten million men were inducted into the military.

When Stan was drafted he chose to serve in the navy. He joined many other famous athletes, actors, singers, and writers who fought during World War II. They left the fame of ball fields and Hollywood to protect and defend their country.

Famous actor Jimmy Stewart served as a pilot and flew 20 combat missions over Germany.

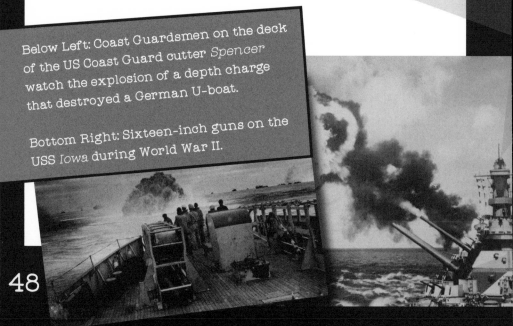

Below Left: Coast Guardsmen on the deck of the US Coast Guard cutter *Spencer* watch the explosion of a depth charge that destroyed a German U-boat.

Bottom Right: Sixteen-inch guns on the USS *Iowa* during World War II.

Ted Williams swearing into the navy in 1942.

Hollywood director Mel Brooks was a combat engineer who had to defuse mines and bombs. And the famous movie star Douglas Fairbanks Jr. did top secret work in North Africa, France, and Sicily.

Yankee catcher Yogi Berra and Red Sox shortstop Pee Wee Reese both served in the navy just like Stan. Yankee Joe DiMaggio served in the army, and Boston Red Sox slugger Ted Williams served in the Marines. Over 500 major league ballplayers and 2,000 minor league players served in the military during World War II.

With so many men leaving to fight overseas, owners of baseball parks were worried that they wouldn't have any teams for the fans to watch. They decided to start the All-American Girls Professional Baseball League. They recruited

Above Left: Actor Douglas Fairbanks Jr.
Above Right: Actor Jimmie Stewart

women's softball players from around
the country and held tryouts. There were
280 young women invited to the finals in
Chicago, and just 60 selected to play on the
first women's professional baseball team.
In 1943, the first year of the league, there
were four teams: the Kenosha Comets, the
Racine Belles, the Rockford Peaches, and the
South Bend Blue Sox. The girls signed major
league contracts and were paid between
$45 and $85 per week.

The girls were expected to play ball wear-
ing skirts and kneesocks. They were taught
how to wear makeup and style their hair

and were required to attend charm school in the evenings. It was a whole different kind of training than the men's ball teams.

But the girls' teams did draw in the fans. They knew how to hit, run, and catch. Fans filled the stadiums to watch. By the end of World War II they had an annual attendance of over 900,000.

With the fighting over, superstars like Stan Musial, Joe DiMaggio, and Yogi Berra returned to their teams and made head-lines for their record-breaking hitting and catching. While baseball fans had enjoyed the girls' teams, they considered them a nov-elty and after the war were ready to return to watching their regular teams. The All-American Girls Professional Baseball League disbanded in 1954.

V-J Day celebrations, August 14, 1945

52

★ CHAPTER ★
FOUR

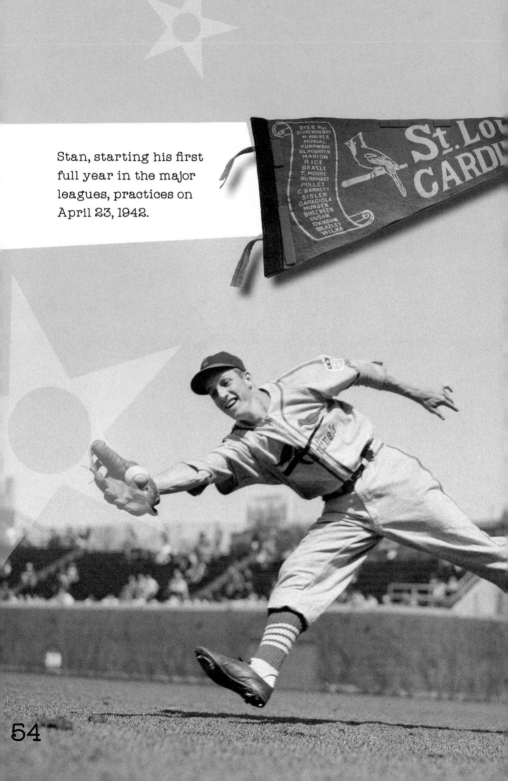

Stan, starting his first full year in the major leagues, practices on April 23, 1942.

For the next two years war raged around the world as Germany and Japan fought the Allies. More and more ballplayers were called into military service. The Cardinals lost outfielders Terry Moore and Enos Slaughter. Their pitchers Johnny Beazley and Howie Pollet also went to serve in the war. With so many team veterans called away, Stan took on more and more of a leadership role for the team.

His calm demeanor and constant positive attitude helped when the players were feeling nervous or defeated. Stan was good at cheering and encouraging his fellow players, and the club managers considered Stan one of their biggest assets. Stan loved his job. He loved baseball and his team. He was always willing to work and practice to improve his skills. He was willing to do whatever it took to win.

And winning was what the Cardinals knew how to do. In both 1943 and 1944 Stan and the Cardinals won the National League pennant and played in the World Series. In 1943 they met their old enemies the New York Yankees. This time the Yankees got revenge on the Redbirds and won the World Series 4-1. But in 1944 Stan and the Cardinals were back on top. They played an all–St. Louis World Series, battling it out against the St. Louis Browns. The Cardinals beat the Browns 4-2.

Stan's batting and fielding were constantly improving, and the fans recognized his skill. He was elected

to the All-Star team both years. In 1943 his batting average was an amazing .357 and only slightly lower in 1944 at .347. In 1943 Stan was the number one batter in the National League, and in 1944 he was only beaten out by Dixie Walker from the Brooklyn Dodgers.

During the off-season, Stan continued to work at the steel mill in Donora. Major league baseball salaries were not high enough to provide a full year's worth of living expenses. Most major league players worked another job during the off-season. Stan felt he was lucky to be able to go back to Donora and have a job waiting for him.

During the winter of 1943, Stan put on his fur parka and traveled to Alaska and the Aleutian Islands. He was part of a group of professional ballplayers who entertained the troops. They gave speeches about baseball, showed World Series movie clips, answered questions, and signed baseballs. Stan loved meeting the servicemen and was happy that he could brighten their day.

In December 1944 Stan and Lil welcomed a new addition to their family—their daughter Geraldine. Stan was a proud papa with little Dickie and daughter Gerri. That made it all the harder to leave when he was called up by the military draft board. It was time for Stan to report for service.

Stan at Naval Training Center
Providence, RI, January 23, 1945

57

Stan with other recruits during basic training at the Bainbridge Naval Training Center in Bainbridge, Maryland, in January 1945.

He chose to join the navy and reported for duty in January 1945. By June he was working in Hawaii, where his job was to run a ferry out to the damaged ships entering Pearl Harbor and bring the crews in to shore. On his afternoons off, he played baseball with the navy's eight-team league to keep his skills sharp.

Then in January 1946, he received the hard news that his father was desperately ill. The navy gave him emergency leave to visit his dad. Stan rushed home to Donora and was relieved to find his father was improving. His dad did survive but never fully recovered. He died two years later.

Once Stan was back on the mainland, he was assigned to the Philadelphia Navy Yard. He served there until he

American Steel and Wire Company's open hearth steel factory in Donora

was discharged in March 1946 at the end of the war.

Stan was back in baseball for the 1946 season. Lil and Dickie were excited to have Stan back home, but Stan had been gone so long that baby Geraldine didn't really remember her daddy. It only took a few weeks before Geraldine decided that her teasing, harmonica-playing father was a pretty fun guy.

By the middle of May, Stan's bat was on fire. He had a .388 batting average and fans were expecting a hit almost every time he came up to bat. The Cardinals' arch nemesis in the National League was the Brooklyn Dodgers. Even the Dodgers fans were impressed by Stan's batting. When Stan came to the plate, the Dodger fans chanted, "Here comes the man! Here comes the man!"

Soon sportswriters across the country dubbed him Stan "The Man" Musial. It was a nickname he would have for the rest of his life. And it was a nickname that made Stan smile.

That summer the Cardinals new manager, Eddie Dyer, began talking to Stan about moving to first base. Stan liked playing outfield and didn't really want to make the change, but one day he opened his locker and found a brand-new first baseman's glove. Stan took the hint and began practicing for first base. Stan was willing to move if it would benefit the team.

That season the Cardinals tied with the Dodgers for first place in the National League. It was the first time the

THE 1946 WORLD CHAMPION ST. LOUIS CARDINALS
Top row (left to right): Nippy Jones, if.; Dick Sisler, of.; Clyde Kluttz, c.; Howard Krist, p.; Del Rice, c.; Ken Burkhart, p.; Trainer Harrison Weaver; Ted Wilks, p.; Joe Garagiola, c.; Blix Donnelly, p. (finished season with Phils); Harry Brecheen, p.; Joffre Cross, if.
Middle row: Fred Schmidt, p.; Walter Sessi, of.; Johnny Beazley, p.; Red Schoendienst, 2b.; Harry Walker, of.; Bill Endicott, of.; Howie Pollet, p.; Erv Dusak, of.; Ken O'Dea, c. (finished season with Braves); John Grodzicki, p.; Red Barrett, p.
Lower row: Marty Marion, ss.; Whitey Kurowski, 3b.; Stan Musial, 1b.; Al Brazle, p.; Coach Buzzy Wares, Manager Eddie Dyer, Coach Mike Gonzalez, Buster Adams, of.; Terry Moore, of.; Enos Slaughter, of.; Murry Dickson, p. Seated in front: Batboys Bob Scanlon and Eddie Dyer, Jr. (Photo by Press Association)

National League had a playoff for the championship. It was to be a best-of-three series. With the help of Stan's triple in the first game and a double in the second game, the Cardinals beat the Dodgers in two games. The Redbirds went on to win the World Series against the Boston Red Sox. Stan got six hits and four RBIs. He won the National League's Most Valuable Player Award and ended the season with a batting average of .365. He had truly earned his nickname Stan the Man.

But the spring of 1947 was awful for Stan. He couldn't hit the ball. He had a batting average of .146 and to top it off he felt terrible. He felt sapped of all strength and when he tried to run it felt like he was dragging weights behind him.

When he became feverish, the team doctor diagnosed him with appendicitis and tonsillitis. No wonder he had been feeling so sick. He was!

The doctor recommended surgery to remove both the appendix and tonsils, but Stan said he wanted to finish the season. After several days of rest, Stan returned to his job at first base. He felt better and began hitting. He ended the season with a .312 batting average, but the Cardinals lost the National League pennant to the Dodgers. Stan was disap-

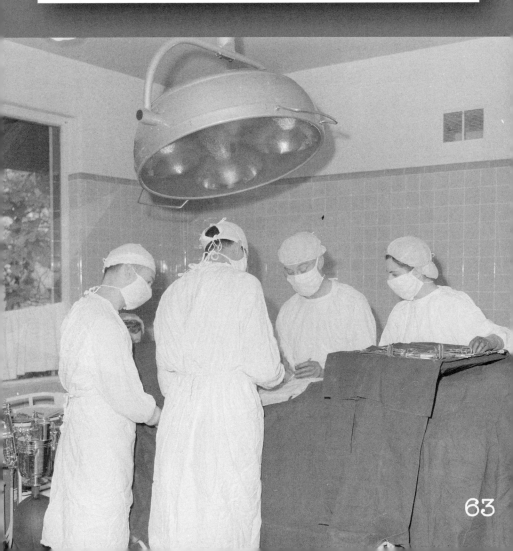

pointed with the loss and said the only thing he liked losing was his appendix and tonsils. He had surgery as soon as the season ended so he'd be ready to play in the spring.

The 1947 season was not memorable to Stan for his playing performance, but it was a landmark season for the major leagues. In April Jackie Robinson joined the Brooklyn Dodgers and became the first African American to play in the major leagues since 1879. In July of the same year, the Cleveland Indians hired Larry Doby, an African American center fielder, and the St. Louis Browns brought on Hank Thompson, a third baseman who was also African American. Professional baseball was officially integrated.

Some white players still believed in segregation, especially players who had grown up in the South. But many players welcomed the change. Stan remembered the time his high school teammate Grant Gray had been discriminated against. He didn't ever want to see anyone treated that way again. He wanted people of all ethnic backgrounds to be given a fair chance and treated with respect. Stan was never one for speechmaking, so it's not unusual that he didn't make speeches in favor of integrating baseball. Stan did what he always did. He quietly led by example and was welcoming and cordial to ballplayers of every color.

Jackie Robinson

68

WHO'S WHO

Professional baseball has been a part of America since 1871, but it has seen quite a few changes over the years. When Stan Musial played the game there were just 16 professional teams in the United States. Today there are 30 teams, with 15 in the National League and 15 in the American League.

When Stan was playing, the St. Louis Cardinals and St. Louis Browns were the farthest west of any baseball teams. And all baseball teams were segregated. Only white players were allowed to play in the American and National Leagues. There was a separate league for black players called the Negro Baseball League. That changed when Jackie Robinson joined the Brooklyn Dodgers in 1947 and baseball became the integrated sport it is today.

Over the years rules have changed and evolved to create the game we play today. Before 1857 the game was won when one team scored 21 aces and there were no innings. In 1864 players introduced

1940 American League

Detroit Tigers
Cleveland Indians
New York Yankees
Chicago White Sox
Boston Red Sox
St. Louis Browns
Washington Senators
Philadelphia Athletics

1940 National League

Cincinnati Reds
Brooklyn Dodgers
St. Louis Cardinals
Pittsburgh Pirates
Chicago Cubs
New York Giants
Boston Bees
Philadelphia Phillies

2015 American League

Toronto Blue Jays
New York Yankees
Baltimore Orioles
Tampa Bay Rays
Boston Red Sox
Kansas City Royals
Minnesota Twins
Cleveland Indians
Chicago White Sox
Detroit Tigers
Texas Rangers
Houston Astros
Los Angeles Angels
Seattle Mariners
Oakland Athletics

2015 National League

New York Mets
Washington Nationals
Miami Marlins
Atlanta Braves
Philadelphia Phillies
St. Louis Cardinals
Pittsburgh Pirates
Chicago Cubs
Milwaukee Brewers
Cincinnati Reds
Los Angeles Dodgers
San Francisco Giants
Arizona Diamondbacks
San Diego Padres
Colorado Rockies

the rule that a base runner must touch each base as he rounds the circuit. And in 1872 the ball size and weight were regulated. Before that time, balls were whatever size each team wanted.

Changes in equipment made the game more consistent. For a while in the 1880s bases could be made of either whitened rubber or marble. Sliding into a marble base had to hurt. Bats were allowed to have a flat side until 1893, when the rules changed to require all bats to be round and made entirely of wood.

The cork-center baseball was introduced in 1910. Batters liked the new ball because it would travel farther than the heavy rubber balls. It was easier to hit a home run with the new balls.

One big change occurred after Stan retired and that was the designated hitter rule. Adopted by the American League in 1973, the rule allows teams to have one player bat in place of the pitcher. It's a controversial rule and fans from the American League and the National League still argue about it.

Diagram of a baseball. *Popular Science* magazine, 1910.

Cross-Section of Latest League Baseball

★ CHAPTER ★
FIVE

74

Stan was feeling good. Really good. He'd healed up nicely from his surgeries, and for the first time in a year was totally healthy. He went to spring training ready to work hard and crack the bat. And that's exactly what he did—all season long.

On April 25, 1948, Stan got his 1,000th career hit, and by June his batting average was an amazing .408. Brooklyn Dodgers pitcher Preacher Roe said the only way to get Stan out was to "walk him on four pitches and pick him off first."

As hard as Stan hit, he couldn't lead the Cardinals back to the World Series. They finished second to the Boston Braves. Stan had the best year of his career. He ended the season with a .376 batting average. He had 39 home runs and 131 RBIs and was the first player to ever win three National League Most Valuable Player Awards.

Stan was still hitting and playing hard when the new decade rolled in. In 1951 Stan was named the Major League Player of the Year by the *Sporting News*. In 1952 he cel-

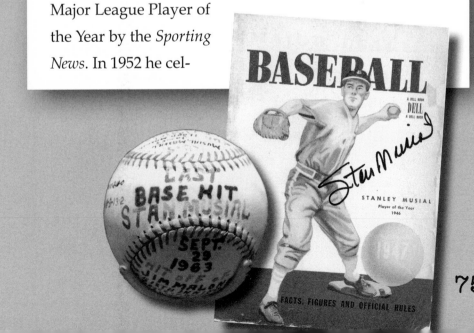

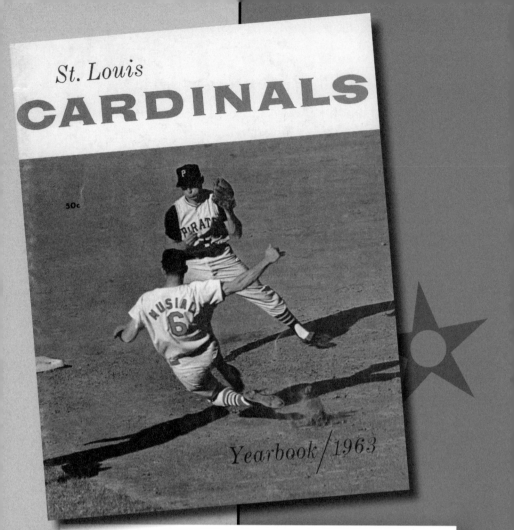

St. Louis
CARDINALS

50¢

MUSIAL
6

Yearbook/1963

ebrated ten years with a batting average over .300. Stan was flattered and embarrassed when baseball legend Ty Cobb was quoted in *Life* magazine as saying, "No man has ever been a perfect ballplayer. Stan Musial, however, is the closest to being perfect in the game today. . . . He plays as hard when his club is way out in front as he does when they're just a run or two behind."

Stan did play hard, but he never made it back to the World Series. The Cardinals would not appear in another World Series until 1964, the year after Stan retired.

Still, the decade of the 1950s was one of triumph for Stan and his baseball skills. He worked hard and stayed healthy so that he could play in every game possible. His strong work ethic paid off, and in 1957 he tied a National League record by playing in his 822nd consecutive ball game. Stan believed that good ballplayers kept playing through hitting slumps, sore muscles, and head colds. He continued playing in every game until August 23, 1957, when he fractured a bone in his left shoulder and had to wait until September 8 to play again. He had been in every Cardinals game from the end of the 1951 season until August 8, 1957.

"THE MAN" WITH A FORMER MANAGER, Billy Southworth, at a reunion of the 1942 Cardinals held last summer.

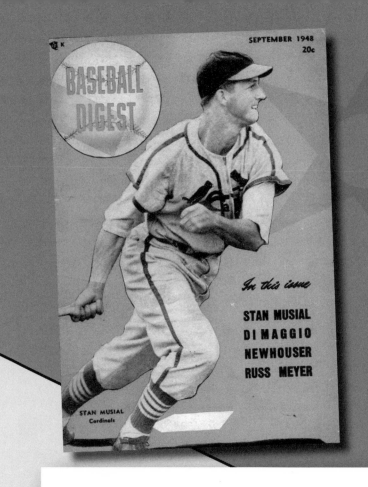

SEPTEMBER 1948
20c

BASEBALL DIGEST

In this issue

STAN MUSIAL
DI MAGGIO
NEWHOUSER
RUSS MEYER

STAN MUSIAL
Cardinals

The next year Stan was rewarded by Cardinals management with a $100,000 contract. It was one of the first $100,000 contracts ever awarded in National League history. Stan also got his 3,000th hit in 1958. He wanted desperately to get the hit at home in St. Louis for his hometown crowd. He even joked about getting walked in every game until he got back to St. Louis so he could make his fans happy. But Cardinals fans were still thrilled when Stan got hit number 3,000 on May 13 at Chicago's Wrigley Field.

Griesedieck
Bros.

Radio star Harry Caray announced the play-by-play saying, "Line drive! Into left field! Hit number three thousand! A run has scored! Musial around first, on his way to second with a double. Holy Cow! He came through!"

When Stan arrived back home, he was met at the train station by a thousand adoring fans. It was a night he would always remember.

The 1958 season had been full of success for Stan, but he wasn't able to repeat his performance the next year. He started out the 1959 season with

80

81

a miserable one hit in fifteen at bats. Stan was mad at himself. He hadn't trained as hard as he should have in the off-season and he was paying for it. Stan worked his way back into shape and back into hitting. He managed to slug out enough home runs to become the first major league player to ever hit 400 home runs and 3,000 hits. He was selected for the sixteenth time to play in the All-Star Game and finished the season with a .255 batting average.

Because he felt he had played so badly in the 1959 season, Stan told the Cardinals management that he would take a $20,000 pay cut for the 1960 season. He felt it was only fair that the Cardinals not pay for performance that was not up to his previous standards. It is hard to imagine that any of today's professional athletes would volunteer to take a pay cut because of one bad year. But that's what Stan did.

Stan continued to keep his body in shape. At the ripe old age of 40, he had to work hard to keep up with his 20-year-old teammates, but Stan did it. In 1960 his batting average was a decent .275. In 1961 he upped it to .288, and in 1962 he was back to a .330 batting average. He was third place in the National League batting standings.

Stan shown waiting on deck for his final at bat.

On Deck for Farewell Performance   Continued

Stan salutes fans on September 29, 1963, during ceremonies marking his final day as a player.

In 1963, at the age of 42, Stan made his twentieth All-Star appearance. At the end of the season he had a solid .255 batting average, but Stan knew in his heart that it was time to hang up his cleats. He played twenty-two seasons in the major leagues with the St. Louis Cardinals and was considered to be one of the greatest and most consistent hitters in baseball history. At the team picnic on August 12, 1963, Stan announced he would retire from the game he loved. Cardinal Nation felt a deep sadness descend upon its fans.

Augie Busch, the Cardinals owner, declared that the Cardinal jersey number six would be forever retired in honor of Stan Musial. It was the first jersey the franchise ever declared retired.

When Stan retired he held or shared seventeen major league records including the career leader in extra-base hits (1,377), games played (3,026), and runs batted in (1,951). Musial was never ejected from a game. It was a record to be proud of, and Stan felt he had finished his career with integrity. But baseball wasn't quite done with Stan. He may have retired from playing baseball but he never left the game.

FOR THE RECORD

When Stan the Man retired he had hit and played his way into the record books.

- Batted .331 in his career, won seven National League batting titles, and led the league in hits six times.
- Ranked first in National League history in hits (3,630) and second in homers (475) when he retired.
- Never ejected in 3,026 regular-season games.
- Played in a record 24 consecutive All-Star Games and hit an All-Star record six home runs.
- Set the National League record for most years (17) and most consecutive years (16) batting .300 or better (50 or more games).

- Set the record for most seasons with one club—3,026 games and 22 years as a Cardinal.
- Established the major league record for most seasons leading his league in doubles (eight) and in extra-base hits (seven).
- Holds National League marks for most seasons leading the league in runs scored (five), in triples (five), and in fewest strikeouts (four).
- Hit five home runs in a May 2, 1954, doubleheader vs. the New York Giants, setting the major league mark for most homers in a twin-bill.

Stan holding the bat commemorating his 300th home run.

★ CHAPTER ★
SIX

Stan, now a vice president with the team, goes through physical exercises with the rest of the team at the beginning of spring training in March 1964.

When Stan took off his number six jersey, he traded it for a suit and tie and began working as a vice president for the St. Louis Cardinals organization. He traveled representing the team, making public appearances, and problem-solving for the franchise.

Then in 1964 he got an offer he couldn't refuse. President Lyndon B. Johnson wanted Stan to serve as the national physical fitness advisor. As a baseball hero, children across America looked up to Stan and listened when he encouraged them to be involved in sports and get regular exercise. Parents and teachers also enjoyed learning from Stan about eating healthy and keeping in shape.

At the beginning of the 1967 baseball season, the Cardinals needed a new general manager. The 1966

general manager, Bob Howsam, unexpectedly left the Cardinals to work for the Cincinnati Reds. It left owner Augie Busch scrambling to find someone the players trusted. Stan stepped up to the plate. He agreed to be the general manager and help out his good friend Red Schoendienst. Being a manager was not Stan's favorite job, but just like in his player days, he dug in and did what he had to do to learn the job. If he had questions, he asked for help. He worked hard to have good relations with the Cardinals players and they loved him for it. With Red managing the games and Stan working with players and their contracts, they had a good year—a championship year.

The Cardinals celebrated their first full year in brand-new Busch Stadium by winning the World Series against the Boston Red Sox 4-3. Stan was thrilled to help manage stellar players like Lou Brock, Orlando Cepeda, and Bob Gibson. He was also happy to return to his regular work as an ambassador for the Cardinals and managing his various business interests.

Stan invested in and managed restaurants and hotels. He gave a great deal of time to charities like the Easter Seals Society, St. Louis Crippled Children, and the Muscular Dystrophy Association.

Stan always enjoyed spending time with his wife, Lil, and their four children. As the kids grew up and had families of their own, Stan and Lil had fun being the grandparents of eleven grandchildren. He was able to give them all the baseball tips they ever wanted.

One of the biggest thrills of Stan's life came in 1969 when he was elected to the Baseball Hall of Fame. Stan was voted in on his very first year of eligibility, with his name appearing on 93.2 percent of the ballots. Attending the induction ceremonies became a tradition for Stan. He tried to be there

every year. The players loved having Stan there and he often opened the ceremonies by playing "Take Me Out to the Ballgame" on his harmonica.

Stan continued to promote Cardinals baseball and his adopted hometown of St. Louis for the rest of his life.

97

The fans of St. Louis never forgot Stan and gave standing ovations whenever he appeared at the ballpark. Stan made his final appearance in front of the Cardinal fans on October 17, 2012. He was 91 years old and he came out riding in a golf cart to wish his team well in game four of the National League Championship Series. The fans went crazy chanting, "Stan the Man!"

Stan died at the age of 92. His wife, Lil, died just eight months before Stan. They were married for almost 72 years. Thousands of Stan's fans went out in the bitter January cold for his visitation. They wanted the world to know that Stan the Man would not be forgotten.

A statue of Stan Musial stands outside the Cardinals' Busch Stadium. The quote on the statue explains how the fans of Stan Musial feel.

Here stands baseball's perfect warrior.
Here stands baseball's perfect knight.

Right: The Stan Musial statue
outside Busch Stadium in St. Louis

MUSIAL

SEBALL LIBRARY

100

Stan was visibly shaken during his induction
into the National Baseball Hall of Fame on
July 28, 1969, in Cooperstown, New York.

President Barack Obama awarding
Stan the Presidential Medal of
Freedom on Tuesday, February 15, 2011,
in the East Room of the White House.

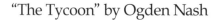

"The Tycoon" by Ogden Nash

The business life of Mr. Musial
is, to say the least, unusual.
First base, outfield, restaurant, bank,
All are home to Stanley Frank.
One moment, slugger of lethal liners,
The next, mine host to hungry diners,
And, between the slugging and the greeting,
To the bank for a directors' meeting.
Yet no one grudges success to Stan,
Good citizen and family man,
Though I would love to have his job—
One half tycoon, one half Ty Cobb.

Source: *Life* magazine (September 5, 1955)

St. Louis Cardinals world
championship pennants flying
over Busch Stadium in St. Louis.

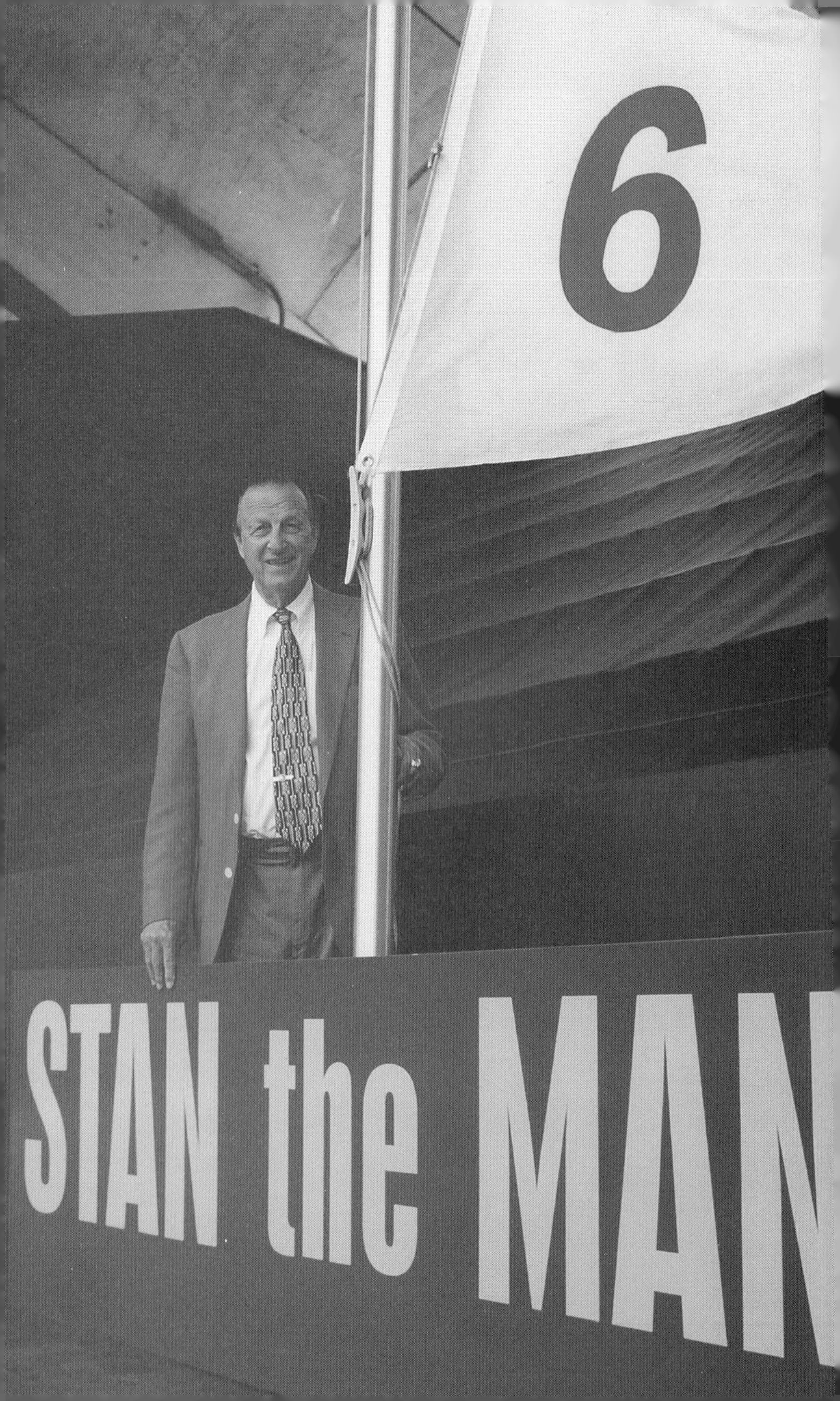
6
STAN the MAN